Artemis:
The People's Priestess

Cora Greenhill

Artemis
The People's Priestess

Cora Greenhill

Three Drops Press
Sheffield, England

First published in 2017 by Three Drops Press

Copyright © Cora Greenhill 2017

All rights reserved. This book or any portion thereof may not be reproduced or used in any manner whatsoever without the express written permission of the publisher except for the use of brief quotations in a book review or scholarly journal.

Cora Greenhill has asserted her right to be identified as the author of this book in accordance with the Copyright, Designs and Patents Act, 1988.

Three Drops Press
Sheffield, United Kingdom

www.threedropspoetry.co.uk

ISBN 978-1-326-98495-3

Cover image used under the terms of the CC0 public domain license.

*To Hannah Frances,
my granddaughter, for being her amazing self.*

'I am, thou woost, yet of the company
A maide, and love hunting and venerye
And for to walken in the wodes wild
And noght to ben a wyf and be with child.'

— **Chaucer**

'Artemis was called a mannish woman and her brother Apollo a womanish man. These twins are a complete quaternity whose union is heavenly: like the sun and moon they pursue and flee and reflect each other-but never touch.'

— **Nor Hall: The Moon and the Virgin**

'Those who are responsible about not allowing creatures to manifest through them, so that they may care for the already manifest, are priestesses of Artemis.'

— **Asia Shepsut: Journey of the Priestess**

'Unlike many surrounding cultures the island of Crete was not invaded until c1,500 BC, and so it offers a unique insight into how a Neolithic culture evolved without disruption into a Bronze aged one while retaining its belief in the unity of life.'

— **Baring and Cashford: The Myth of the Goddess**

'Here and here alone...the human bid for timelessness was disregarded in the most complete acceptance of the grace of life the world has ever known.'

— **quoted in Baring and Cashford: The Myth of the Goddess**

Frontispiece: Spring 1450 BC	13
In the Gold of Flesh	13
Characters in order of speaking	15
Prelude: Winter 1450BC	17
Greek merchants onboard a ship leaving Crete	18
PART 1	23
Tsunami	24
New Order	25
Second Sight	26
Double trouble	27
Party over	29
Little Boy Lost	30
Toddler Troubles	31
Gotcha!	33
Basic curricular	34
Tall Stories	36
For the record	37
Legal Highs	39
PART 2	41
Wild Child	42
Father's Daughter	43
He tried!	45
Mother Wit	46
Displacement Activity	50
Medicine Way	51
Wild Rite	53
First Dance	54

Bunking off	55
Menarche Rite	56
Wild diplomacy	57
Booty	60
Upwardly Mobile	61
Girltalk	62
Rap attack	64
Taking a stand	66
Beyond the Pale	67
PART 3	69
The Return	70
Arrival	72
Meeting her match	75
Taming the shrew	76
Catching up with the times	79
Having it Made	83
Beyond Narcissism	84
Family	88
The last sibling spat	90
Fate	96
Postlude	98
Explanatory notes on names and places	101
Glossary	103
Thanks to	105
About the Author	106

Frontispiece: Spring 1450 BC

In the Gold of Flesh

Picture her as they did
at those last Spring Rites:
a ribbed cone of light, prickly with energy,
spinning earthwards, called by the drone
of the hive, drawn by the thick scent,
the whirr of moving air.
And the hopeful Zan, soaring sky high
in Leto's honeyed thighs
crying loud for her.

She required
this spiralling together,
Not just the milk and the honey,
the big breasts bursting for her.
But the white heat, the smelt gold,
the forge of frenzied dance,
to fizz into life,
a cellular starburst.

Characters in order of speaking

Chorus – Priestesses of Knossos

Merchants – Traders from Mainland Greece

Artemis – Priestess of Knossos, daughter of High Priestess Leto, born in Crete on the night of the vast volcanic eruption on Thera that led to the fall of the Minoan World. She becomes disgusted with the foreign ways beginning to dominate, and goes into exile in the mountains, leading and teaching young women in traditional skills such as hunting and gathering, natural medicine, shamanic dance rituals and rites of passage.

Artemis in myth – *One of the 12 Olympian Deities, twin sister of Apollo. Their parents were Leto and Zeus. She became known as Virgin Goddess (Artemis Parthenos), Goddess of the Moon, Huntress, Goddess of the Wild, Goddess of childbirth, and many other titles by the Greeks. Later a fierce and much feared protectress of young girls in Sparta. Her origin may have been as an orgiastic Goddess, or even as the triple Goddess – maiden, mother and crone.*

Apollo (**Paian** as a boy) – Twin brother of Artemis, seduced away from Crete by the Greeks as a young man.

Apollo in Myth – *Although jealous, violent and vengeful, Apollo became known as the God of light, harmony, music and civilsation. He famously killed the sacred python of the Prophetess of Delphi and usurped her famous shrine.*

Paian in myth – *Pre-Greek name of a young God in Crete.*

Maya – Ancient wise-woman and herbalist, childhood friend and teacher of Artemis.

Maya or Maia in myth – *The name is widely used to mean Earth Mother, sometimes in Her Crone aspect.*

Girls of Knossos – Priestesses in training and huntresses.

Rap Chorus – Modernisers.

Kallisto – Childhood friend, lover and soulmate of Artemis.

Kallisto/Callisto in myth – *An ancient Cretan Goddess pre-dating Artemis, who was later pictured famously by Titian as the follower of Artemis who was punished by her for becoming pregnant after being seduced by Zeus.*

Daphne – Priestess working with Kallisto.

Hyacinthos – Young priest of Knossos, seduced by Apollo.

Hyacinthos in myth – *Originally a young flower God, precursor of Narcissus, later a beautiful young prince with whom Apollo fell in love.*

Prelude: Winter 1450BC

Greek merchants onboard a ship leaving Crete

Merchant 1

You've missed a treat, lad!
You'll never see the like of Knossos again.
The shrines of the temple are groaning with gold.
All expertly worked into those queer axes
and bulls' heads and bees and such. Very quaint,
but the metal is priceless. Then there's the oil,
and we're not talking olive oil here, or almond.
We're talking iris, we're talking jasmine,
We're talking very expensive perfume.

Merchant 2

Look! Even the jars are carved from onyx.
Onyx! Do you know what that costs?
And each contains the oil from a stremata
of flowers. Perfumeries work through
summer days, and into the night, they say,
pressing, distilling – methods top secret, 'course.

Merchant 1

For the moment! Someone will crack,
some little prat will sell out in the end.
Liquid's pricier, weight for weight, than gold
– it's all supply and demand!

Merchant 3

But Knossos – you know – what's it like?

Merchant 2

Entertainment world-class, accommodations 5-star.
The talent delish in every way – far outstripped
highest expectations.

Merchant 3

And the girls half-stripped as well, they say?

(Guffaws)

Merchant 4

But jewelled like queens!
Their dresses beggar belief,
But…it's their eyes that you see…
they seem to shine from inside,
It's like they've nothing to hide,
and nothing…to fear…know what I mean?

Merchant 1

Undressed to kill, aye.

Merchant 3

Well stacked too, we've heard!

(Louder guffaws)

Merchant 2

Slender and curvaceous, aye, but strong as men.
The girls compete with boys on equal terms
in all the games. They cross dress, too,
the lads and lasses…aprons…codpieces…

Merchant 3

They won't play hard to get then!
I'd give it them, if they let me onshore.
Did you all break into the…inner sanctum?

Merchant 4

Hey, lad, listen up. These...women,
the temple ladies...Potnia's priestesses...
passed among us, all through the day.
Always on a mission, organising,
advising, but ... graceful...
always smiling...like it's all...a dance.
They still hold sway in all the offices...but
how can I put it? They want to understand us,
like there's no right or wrong, just
differences they haven't met before.
But that's in the public places.
Further in...deep in the labyrinth...
you have to be invited...initiated
...hard to describe it...first dark then light...
first closed, then open to the sky,
mysterious, but safe...you open up
...the rituals, strange but somehow familiar...
you're bathed...in water, yes, but
something else. You lose yourself,
come out changed, re-arranged.
It's not for everyone of course...
there's a holy power...

Merchant 3

And they dance like dervishes, there, yeah?

Merchant 4

No, just try to picture this...the tiled floor
they dance on, shines like the western sky,
when sun's just slid away. And woven o'er
and o'er with devious designs,
that guide the lines in a labyrinthine dance.
I swear it blows your mind,
puts you in a kind of trance,

if you try to follow them as they glide,
spiralling in and out, in circles
tight then wide. It's fair hypnotic.

Merchant 3

'specially with the Knossos wine in you!

Merchant 4

Listen, you can get drunk on the temple air:
the breath of night's all rich with perfumes rare.
There are scented pools where you can bathe...

Merchant 3

C'mon, Jason, did you get laid?

Merchant 4

Brother, I...was chosen, I don't know why,
to be initiated in a most ecstatic way.
I drank my fill from a fine lady's cup
of such strong wine, I doubt
I'll ever quench my thirst again...

(crude cheers)

Merchant 3

Not with this rank beer!

Several voices

Say no more, brother, say no more.

A single voice

Holy cow!

> *(A massive rumble and deafening roar is heard, then crashing and screaming as the ship is rocked/wrecked by a tsunami.)*

PART 1

Tsunami

Chorus 1

Velkanos, the smouldering peak of Thera, ejaculated
his pillar of fire into the Aegean night so high
it was seen by the whole known world. Then waves
high as the hills, laid waste Crete's fertile plains.

When the density of that world-altering night
finally slackened into the twilight of a noxious
dawn, temples lay flattened, fleets sunk,
and half the clans of Keftiou had been swept away.

New Order

Mycenean warlord

You couldn't have planned it.
Crete was the ultimate prize!
Central to all trade routes.
natural disasters are natural allies
for bringing down Empires,
especially when the victims
have no defences. They relied
on the sea to protect them –
it turned against them big time.
Now infrastructure decimated.
Fleets, most of their men, eradicated.
Only Knossos survived intact,
but ruling priesthood traumatised.
Terrible loss of course.
Valuable real estate messed up,
crops and property destroyed.
But a starving population,
easy to coerce, convert, control.
Lost their faith in whatever it was
they believed in – Potnia, I think
they called it. We'd soon put
the fear of Gods in them,
make them dance to our tune.

Second Sight

Chorus 2

But in Eileuthia's sacred cave, stranded
on empty breasts, a newborn girl. Her cries
drowned by her mother's still-labouring groans.
Another, a brother, to be born.

The spirit of the Goddess entered the infant girl,
empowered her to assist. She willed
the boy to live, heard his first plangent cries,
more like warbling songs, than wailing.

Perhaps her prophetic soul already knew
these songs would charm a new world into being.
But soon she would find that her unnatural toil
had midwifed her own nemesis, her foil.

Double trouble

Artemis

Whatever. Yep, there were two of us,
me and my little bruvver, Paian then – Apollo
only later, when he'd become the darling
of the foreigners: a swerver and a traitor.

But two weeks prem, we were sorry
specimens back then, clinging to each other
in the clammy cave that saved us
from a baptism of red-hot pumice.

We'd been shucked into the darkest dark
the world has ever known,
just missing the biggest fireworks ever seen.
Labour induced by shock: the roar

like Earth herself in labour.
I always suffered from tinnitus,
especially when arguments started.
And girl, did they rage!

I wouldn't let go of him, so he survived
and wouldn't let go of me. Original
co-dependency. Start and end of story.
Could neither split nor live in harmony.

The rest is history. Well, Greek mythology,
actually: original spin. Before they invented
philosophy and democracy,
they had to pull the plug on the back story.

Millennia of so-called pre-history
almost lost without trace that night
as our mother Leto staggered and slogged
through a sick-making fog,

clinging to her two pack of brats,
howling from hunger and cold.
Vultures were bloated from the rotting bodies
of the drowned, or we'd likely not have made it.

Party over

Chorus 1

And she found a stage set for a play
that would never be performed.
The Solstice feast was spread: knives and ladles
poised. Fires had been laid, tiles polished,
altars adorned. Great jars of extra virgin
lined the walls. Air thick with aromas
of honey, mead, sticky sultanas,
and a stench of overripe cheese.
Ground almonds, chestnuts,
heaps of barley for beer...and *krassi*
of course, still young, but a promising year.
Herds bleated complaints in their pens,
teats aching and hard.
Boars and deer and all the surrendered ones,
dripped blood in the well-cooled larders.
Bulls were corralled for the Games.
The dancers knew their steps,
kouretes their leaps and turns,
pipers their tunes.

Chorus 2

Not a stone of the temple had fallen,
not a drop had been spilled from her urns.
Apart from shock, and hacking coughs,
the people of Knossos were unharmed.
But the clans, whose party it was,
would never arrive.
And the priesthood was paralysed.

The twins were seized on as first signs
of Earth's appeasement: a rainbow
in a hurricane of despair.

Little Boy Lost

Apollo

She got tinnitus, I got labyrinthitis!
The chaos of Knossos permanently
affected my balance.
All those gloomy, twisting corridors!
All that drama and despair!
All that groaning and moaning
coming through the walls.
My infancy was purgatory.
Men all drowned at sea in the tsunami.
Little brother, smother smother.
All those great breasts and little me
all dressed up with nowhere to go.
Their labyrinth was just a bloody maze
to me – full of dead ends.
I never did get mystery.

I was always attracted to clean:
clean lines would be the hallmark
of all my designs. None of your winding,
underground passageways in mine.

Toddler Troubles

Artemis

Leto left right after she'd dropped us
off at Knossos. Never saw her again,
except in dreams, always the ash grey
of those days that greeted our birth.

But losing the slippery grip of our pre-natal
embrace, we'd reacted in different ways
bruvver and me. I was the strong one,
denying my needs you might say.

He just demanded attention:
well, adoration actually.
Buckets of it preferably,
which is all fine and dandy in infancy.

But his sense of inferiority led to vanity,
made him a sucker for the flattery
of foreigners. He became their celebrity,
and ultimately, of course, a so-called divinity.

Ironic really, he was such a weakling.
I was running after four-legged things
since I could toddle on two. My first
real spring – after three years of winter –

bloomin' great! Blossom knee-deep,
grass over my head, butterflies! Oh my!
Swallows and swifts getting all acrobatic –
I was ecstatic! Little bruvver not so.

Still unsteady on his pegs, wails
when he sees me shoot away
in pursuit of some lizard or bat.
Our nurses do their best to distract.

But when he falls and I see him stuck
to the ground with his chubby arms up,
I just have to stop in my tracks,
and go back. Paian, my ruddy baby.

Gotcha!

Apollo

God! How I hated those picnics
where flies got in your food!
Made me into a serial killer
of creepy crawly things
– expert at pulling off wings,
de-scaling, dismembering –
ignoring my sister's pleas.

Then they taught us both archery,
but she always had the edge on me –
uncanny, how she hit that bullseye.
Some kind of women's sorcery.

But I had my music: there at least
I could boast mastery.
No one could take that from me.
Ever. Hence my immortality.
They called my playing heavenly:
natural then I should become a God…

Basic curricular

Artemis

Hmm. You've probably seen him pictured
in that radiant glow – a halo of sunshine
behind him: God! So unsubtle.
And that absurd chariot of fire!

To give him his due, he was a cool musician:
one of the few to make you sit up and listen.
In a class of his own – or so one hears
(from him – never one to celebrate his peers).

But 'Father of Civilisation'! Do me a favour!
Proportion and harmony: basic curricular
subjects in Knossos. Elementary. Easy peasy.
We'd taught it for generations, even to Myceneans.

You want to see genius? Take my friend Diktynna.
An original, a seer of patterns, a weaver
of webs. She had an uncanny knack
of making things work that shouldn't.

Could be a twist in the handle of a jug,
cross-lacing the breast of a dress,
lighting the angle of a stair – whatever
she turned her hand to showed her signature flair.

A visionary, but totally pragmatic,
her consultancy style was somewhat Socratic:
she'd challenge the very premises of engineers
restoring bridges and harbour piers.

But all the time, with her innate diplomacy
and generosity, she'd welcome new ideas,
so passing on our open-minded legacy.
She was truly a mother of democracy!

Oops, I've used the big D word the Greeks
are so proooud of – as if they invented it!
Reduced it, actually, to a fraction of the population –
discounting women and all our non-human relations.

Tall Stories

Apollo

When the Hellenes took an interest in me
as a slip of a lad, what should I say?
Theirs was the rising star.
I started to get creative
about the circumstances of my birth.
Said I wasn't Keftian at all,
had been born in the dark to bring light.
Bigged up my brilliance.
Backed up by my dazzling blond looks,
they bought the story, and even I
began to believe it. As I began
to believe in their Gods.

For the record

Artemis

You see, they just made things up
to create male supremacy –
's how they invented so-called history.
Wait 'n' I'll put some records straight.

First, they based their Virgin Goddess on me
with about as much accuracy
as they branded our randy Minotaur
a monster, and Pasiphae a perverted whore.

But let's start with me, and that virgin bit –
Artemis Parthenos – ho ho. Ask Sappho.
And those pictures that make me look like
Twiggy in skinny mini-skirt! Let's get real!

I developed to triple D
– considered de rigour in a temple queen.
Oh yes, you're expecting me to say how
they got in the way out hunting!

Actually, that's bollocks – I mean, they do –
get in the way – as any guy who's tried
to run in a kilt will testify. So codpiece design
was state of the art in our time.

Our kidskin bodices gave excellent support:
a match for your 'Shock Absorbers' any day!
And our athletic lifestyle ensured our pecs
could take the strain whatever game we played.

So you can forget another crazy story
about Amazons having surgery
to modify their breasts for archery or war.
That self-harm wasn't militaristic, it was

anti-cosmetic! When foreigners forced marriage
to be the order of the day, disfigurement
reduced their market value you could say:
a drastic way to escape a life of slavery.

Legal Highs

Chorus

For we were people trained in ecstasy –
all acts of pleasure were our rituals.
Through discipline we harnessed energy
for bliss – our compensation for mortality.

We were the first to cultivate the vine,
add honey to the alchemy of wine.
The clans would brew their barley beer
to keep them strong and bring good cheer.

We had no anti-depressants, aspirin or penicillin
but we had opium, saffron and venom –
to soothe our pains, open our inner eye,
keep our subtle bodies electrified.

PART 2

Wild Child

Chorus

The little girl's feet just itched to get out
of the temple. She made friends with folk
who had dirt on their sandals, entered
with baskets and beasts on their backs.

Her favourite was the famous hunter
she called Uncle Zan: she'd weaned herself
from her nurse to stake her claim on his lap.
Pretending to sleep, she'd listen to his stories.

Father's Daughter

Artemis, aged 4

I listen to the hunter's heart,
chunk pum, chunk pum, chunk pum.
I breathedeep to slow my heartbeat
down to his. To make us onething.
His hands warm and heavy on my ribs.
My cheek on his chest, only his thin vest
between us. He smells of wetleaves,
stirredup by houndhooves, and boarblood
drying. I melt into his warmdamp, absorb
his big'n'strong. He thinks I'm asleep,
but I'm safeawake, saferawake,
safer than safe. I'm listening
to his heart. I snuggle deeper,
my knees on his belly. My fingertips
test the springyhair on his arm.
I know without looking its copperycolour
with some silver sprinkled in.
Then by his elbow there's rough
under the hair, like a bigthick scab.
A scab on a grownup? I get scabs
on my knees when I losemygrip
on a tree or skidonscree.
Touching Zan's big scab feels like
touchingme. Suddenly, I get it:
we're made of the samestuff, himandme!
I spring up, straight as an arrow.
'What?' he blinks, dazedawake.
I'm squinting to see the colour of his eyes
in the firelight. Dark, I think,
but not as dark as mine.
'What, Timi?' Zan peers backatme.
'I am Artemis, daughter of Leto
and Zeus - that'll be you.
You'll make me a bow'n'arrows
as strong as Apollo's,
and I'll have hounds

faster than his to follow.
I'll need leather sandals and a tunic.
Oh, and a saffron dress because
I'll also be mistress of the dance.
I'll live mostly in the mountains with girls,
except…when I'm needed to help women
having babies…and stuff like that.'
'Of course, my Lady! I see we have
the gift of prophecy too!'

He tried!

Apollo

See? Even he doted on her – Zan,
Leto's fancy man!
But I'd sussed it as a kid, that I –
and sis – were directly in line
to the Olympian divine.
I knew he'd be Zeus –
they'd make him Top God
to get him onside.
I tried to explain it to Timis,
but was she interested?
She was always a queer one:
all she ever cared about
was feathered or furred.
Only happy charging around in woods,
skin scratched, hair full of burrs.
Her teachers despaired.
Before she was old enough to hunt
if she needed an alibi to stray,
it was Maya, an ancient wisewomen,
who wandered the land – a regular hag.
Art – born a High Priestess mind –
carried her bag!

Mother Wit

Artemis, aged 7

Maya is smoking her pipe. It smells nice.
She knows which plants to grow the smoke
with. She's been walking about
a very long time so she knows everything
and tells me anything I want to know.
Sometimes we sit down and I lean on her.
We don't even talk, but I feel like my mind
is swelling like a pear on a tree,
just filling up with what it needs to know.

Down in the village where we've just been
there's a line of smoke from a fire
like the smoke from Maya's pipe.
I squeeze my eyes so the two lines
come together, to make one line –
so we're still joined to the clan people.
'specially my best friend, Kallisto.
She shoots as well as me. She taught me
how to make arrows, and I gave her my knife.

A question has been gnawing me
like a tree rat on a nut. Today it bursts out:
'Why don't all the children learn the dances?
Why do they have to work all the time,
scraping the soil? Can Kallisto come
to the temple to live with me? Can she?'
Maya went on puffing before she answered,
but I was used to that.

Maya

Maybe she can. Maybe she can.
No one says she can't.
But not all the children can.
Bairns have been born so fast
since so many were lost.

There aren't enough teachers left,
with all the temples destroyed.
And their bellies have to be filled.
We're put here for different reasons, Timis,
different jobs to do. But you're right,
the children deserve better.
Mind you, you don't know what hard jobs
the Lady has in store for you!
Might be even harder than planting barley.
Sounds like it's hard for you already,
just trying to figure things out,
get to the bottom of things: that's hard.

Folk didn't used to live like this.
There was always plenty of food
stored for a dry season. No one gave more
to the temple than they could afford.
Lots of holidays too, feasting and dancing:
everyone went to the temples then!
Festivals for every season –
every person had their share
of mead or barley beer.
No one went hungry or lacked cheer.
So it was. But even then,
things happened we couldn't understand.
Like my own poor wee babby – its spirit
flew off before it could breathe sweet air,
let alone suck from my big breasts,
hard as melons. Oh dear!

Artemis

I thought she was crying,
but Maya laughed till she wobbled
all over and tears streamed
down the gorges of her cheeks.

Maya

Oh! The aching and fever!
No other babbies needing to suckle
that year. That's why I had to take herbs,
to dry up my milk – and once I got interested,
no one could stop me studying plant medicine.
I soon knew more than anyone could teach me.
I was like you. Couldn't stop asking, searching.
So I guess that was why my little one's spirit
fled so quick, to show me my work.
Maybe these clan children will show you yours!
Look – there's one over there! What's he doing
stabbing that ground with his stick?

Artemis

He'll hurt the roots of the chicory plants!
He's splitting the volvoi bulbs!
And crushing hyacinth stems with his feet!

Maya

Ssh! The boy will run off and learn nothing
if he sees you're angry. Let's talk to him kindly.

So young man, how are you today?
You look tired, come, let's sit down here.
Do you know the names of these plants?

Boy

No, Mama. We've been told
to clear them to plant beans.

Maya

But look, there's dictamos here,
just peeking out again!
It hasn't been seen here since the big wave.

Feel how soft it is!
And malotiri, look, and sage there.
You may need their medicine in winter.
Medicine land isn't for beans.
There won't be enough water here
by Solstice anyway: you'd have to carry it
every day from the river.
See this deep blue spire? That's hyssop.
And these are young chaste-trees:
they may flower this year, if we're lucky,
give us very special seeds
that your mothers and sisters will use.

Boy

Where will we sow the beans then?

Maya

Let's look down there by the stream
under the rotting leaves by those walnut trees
there's good rich loam. Just kick away
this leaf mulch – good – you see? Black earth.
Smell that, that's the food beans need.
They'll be in the shade too. But wait
a week or two before you plant - the snow
in the gully just beyond that outcrop
isn't melted yet: there may be more floods
that'll wash the wee roots away.

Artemis

The eyes of the boy went round with respect.
I felt tall beside Maya as he bowed and left.

Displacement Activity

Chorus

No one listened to her childish clamour
to have Kallisto share the temple glamour.
They couldn't afford to create a precedent –
it would open the floodgates to applicants.

Instead, to distract her from her growing rage,
they agreed to allow her, though under-age,
to start to learn to hunt with Uncle Zan,
which proved a most successful plan.

Now every chance she could get
she was out with the chase, the hunters' pet.
Her eyes were sharp and her arrows were true,
her legs so strong she almost flew,
face hot as a faggot, throat dry as July,
she didn't mind. Or she'd crouch for hours,
inviting deer, and boar, and even a bear,
to enter her space, show her their powers.

Medicine Way

Artemis, aged 11

Maya sent for me, and it's strange to walk
in the woods at her pace again, my legs
want to race on ahead. But I hold her hand,
much smaller and softer than I remember,

and carry her bag, that weighs nothing at all,
but she mutters it's all she can do to carry
her own bones now. 'But that's not why
I called you here today,' she wheezes,

grasping my hand tighter, as if I might run away
when I hear what she has to say. I feel
my heart sink, a bit ashamed, and a bit afraid.
But when she speaks, it's not what I think.

'Soon you'll be making your woman's rites.
as you begin to flow with the moon.
You'll be taken care of, helped to choose,
a path, so I don't want to talk about you.

But the May Festivals are coming.
Do you know why they're called orgiastic?'
My stomach turned a somersault.
I didn't want to talk about this,

but my old friend wouldn't let me go.
'You know that not all girls and boys
have the chance to train at the temple.
Remember how you'd rant only last year?

We can't change that yet, but now
there's something you can do.
Far too many babbies are being born,
for wisewomen are few.

Women shouldn't ever conceive
unless a child's soul has agreed.
But there are clansmen, and now Incomers
who haven't learnt to hold their seed.

And the women are so busy growing crops
to feed their families, they're losing
the knowledge of herbs that could stop
their wombs opening for a season.

Those herbs you're carrying are the ones
they need, but they've forgotten how to use them.
They can get sick if they use them wrong.
Will you help me teach them?'

I was silenced. And relieved. She knew
it wasn't me who'd need the herbs,
or be running to the woods at Beltane
with some panting Priestling.

Wild Rite

Artemis, aged 11

The herbs are bubbling noxiously.
The women gossip lewdly.
I grow fidgety. I can hear shouts
from girls beyond the trees.
Kallisto – she must be there.
I catch Maya's eye, she winks,
and I'm free. But it's twilight,
I can hardly see. I tense,
listening. They're hiding!
Thorny briars a dense thicket.
I'm deafened by crickets...then,
giggles from right above me,
and she drops from a branch,
lands on my back. All gangly,
in a mane of tangled hair.
My knees buckle, I crumble.
'Wanna learn to wrestle?'
Black eyes fix mine. 'Come on!'
I let them pin me down easily.
a squirm of skinny girls,
all elbows, knees, long dusty curls.
I laugh till I ache. Then start to shake
as a knee presses between my legs
and my hips rise like a cat's back
and the cry tears through me like an arrow.

First Dance

Artemis and Kallisto, aged 12

Can you hear drums?
The Summer Solstice dancing! It's begun!
C'mon, we'll be late! We tugged at Maya
until she sent us packing, wheezing
and complaining she was far too old to run.
So like hounds off the lead, we shot
straight through the vineyards, veered right
at the West Court to avoid the queues.
Quick wash at the fountain, Kallisto's jaw dropped
when she saw the loos! Unbuckling our tunics,
we tore through the gloom up the back stairs
to the raiment room. Chucked Kallisto a frock,
glanced at the clock, ripped off my jerkin,
pulled on a saffron skirt, swore at the laces
on my kidskin braces. Down the broad stairs
three at a time, past pretty young priestlings,
tweaking their make-up and preening their curls,
their aprons bobbing as they watched the whirling girls,
who swept us off our feet to an Asian-fusion beat,
swirling round the labyrinth: the pounding heart of Crete.

Bunking off

Apollo

Ah yes, the Knossos girls! Highly prized,
but what a price!

Woe betide a guy who tries to taste the treat
before his *kouretes* training is complete!

Not red tape exactly, but a silver thread
so long it weaves you in an endless web

leads you into such dark and spooky places
you could lose your mind and come out crazy.

The path of the initiate is long and steep –
no hoops to jump through, just bulls to leap!

Years of training to get the timing right –
the pay-off they say, is worth it on the night.

I wasn't up for it, (or up to it!) so
I followed the Greek lads I got to know –

was led astray, you might say,
by the men of Mycenae

who, after a day of throwing their weight around,
would quaff wine until late, out on the town,

and for half a crown, with girls they called whores –
I soon found I could make them cry out for more!

Menarche Rite

Artemis, aged 12

It was the day I hadn't waited for!
Kallisto and I had bent the rules,
but I wasn't such a fool
as to pass on the pleasures
of my menarche ritual!

Waxed doors slid shut behind me.
For a heartbeat, I felt trapped!
Relax. Check out the story. Crikey,
they've made this seriously sexy.
Lamplit pools, rouge-plastered
walls, air thick with incense – clary sage,
rose. Hands unwrap me, I'm stark naked
in wet heat. Feathers whisk my skin.
Goosebumps. Nipples harden
– and as for my maidenhair fern!
Warm drink, bitter sweet – well laced that!
A pipe and frame drum play so quietly
the sound seems to come from inside me.
Weak with the drug, I'm lifted as I fall
into a scented bath, float foetal,
eyes half-closed, phantoms in the steam.
Owl perches on a beam of lamplight,
dolphin supports the curve of my back,
hair is water-snakes, arms fins.
Licked all over by tongue of cow, wow!
Then big cats' paws pat me dry.
I find I'm pillowed on fruit of the vine.
Or it may be the wine. Then snakes
glide from these alabaster urns,
coil ankles, glide up thighs.
A sistrum hisses. Snake power
inside me. I stretch, hips sway,
weight of snakes moving me like a woman.
I hold my frame drum, find my own rhythm.

Wild diplomacy

Chorus

After her official initiation,
she didn't wait for an invitation.
Novice of the Priesthood now,
she presented Knossos council
with her petition.

Artemis

'Ladies of the Labyrinth, and all Officiates
of the council of The City of Knossos,

its villages and mansions, farms and forests.
I am the novice Artemis,

here to record a formal application
for your approval, for Kallisto Mavrolakis

from the village clan of Tylissos,
to enter into the Labyrinth of Knossos

as an initiate to the priesthood of Potnia
on my personal recommendation

and the sponsorship of my Uncle Zan,
recent Zeus Welkanos, High Priest.

I understand that historical precedents
allow her this privilege as of right.

Praise be to Potnia and blessed be.'
As I sat down I swear

High Priestess Pasiphae smiled at me.
But then the corn I'd thrown landed

in the fire. Started to pop. I might have known
it'd be Minos to quibble, supercilious git.

Shit! Why couldn't they have found a grown up
to sit on the temple forum, instead of this

adolescent, uninitiated, half-Greek nit?
'Your Graces, I know I'm a mere male...

but it appears that this young lady's...er, sorry,
this novice's request is out of order.

Under the newly established temple
management committee's explicit advice

about the conditions applying in cases...'
...blah blah yawn get to the point!

'Sadly, it is the case that there is a waiting list
of highborn girls entitled to be initiates.'

'They have not been personally recommended
by a member of the temple, nor sponsored by one!'

Ariadne heckled on my behalf. 'They don't need
sponsoring, my dear, they have private means.'

'Since when did the size of one's herds
or looted booty from piracy help one gain access

to temple training?' 'Since the temple can no longer
afford charity – she has to fill her own granaries

or see her people starve!' And on and on,
same old same old new order versus time

out of mind. I sat and waited for the debate
to run its course. I knew interest had abated

when Minos and his cronies started craning
their necks to check the time on the dial

in the light well. 'Suggest motion carried
due to pressure of important AOB,' said he.

All those in favour...and that was it. There was
some muttering of course, 'Bare-faced cheek!'

'Poor labouring family, you know!'
That's rich, from the Mycenean traders' lobby!

But we were home and dry. To be fast-tracked,
ask late on a busy day. Child's play.

Booty

Drunken merchant

It's a buyer's market. What can you do?
We took on board all we wanted of their frippery.
And some capable girls. Easy
to persuade most of them to leave with us.
Nothing for them here but hard graft
and scant rations. The temple
tries to persuade them otherwise
– plays on their loyalty to the priesthood,
and...Potnia – some kind of Goddess...
Not much evidence of Her in the fields!

Mind you, we did get one of those fine girls
from the temple. Minos wanted rid of her –
called her an imposter. Fierce hussy –
didn't come exactly willingly! Fought
like a wild cat actually, I've scratches
to prove it. Kallisto the Cat we call her –
but she's got the looks and carriage – well,
if she comes to her senses, she'll fetch
a high price and make a royal marriage!

Upwardly Mobile

Apollo

I have to admit, teachers at Knossos had been top notch:
their skill was impeccable, nothing was botched.
I'd learnt to expand their principles to great effect,

and Mycenean friends were highly impressed.
I showed them I could make their columns taller,
doorways wider, all that would make them tower above the rest.

So I didn't take much persuading to join a fleet to Greece!
They assured me I'd enjoy the highest prestige,
and a dazzling life of music, luxury and ease.

Girltalk

Several girls' voices

'Hey Themis, what's your hurry?'
'She's got a date with Chloe,' 'Never!'
'Oh, don't worry! It won't last!
Chloe comes far too fast!'

'Whose cup is Helen drinking from tonight?'
 'Poor Hebe's! I hope she's ready for a brawl!
Those hungry hounds have a gentler appetite.
Helen has no patience in the dance at all.'

'You sound as if you've licked her salt yourself!'
'Whose, Helen's? Sure, I've eaten from her plate!
Her food's too hot for Hebe's taste.
Her tongue's forked too: frankly, she's two faced.'

'Ah! You've been the victim of her hit and run?'
'Well…I wouldn't say we didn't have some fun!'
'Who's rowing your boat now? '
'I'm hoping Ganymede will leap my prow!'

 'Isn't he a little…well, too much in demand?
Does he have some special magic in his hands?'
'More of a special way with his magic wand,'
'Ugh! Whatever forks your lightening!'

'Ah! I'd like a whole row of bobbing aprons
to be my welcome party!' 'Two kouretes
on either aching thigh would do for me.'
'Mmm! A little rumpy pumpy before tea!'

'Shhh! There's Artemis! She'll say you're underage!
You know how talk of men's stuff makes her rage!'
She'll sentence you to months of celibacy
out on a mountain eating barley and green tea.'

'Oh Artemis! Come poke my fire with your darts

that never miss! Let me unbuckle your braces,
that hidden loveshaft lick, till it's harder than your heart!
I'll cover those burnished thighs with sloppy kisses,
come with a stream strong as a she-goat pisses.'

'You crazy fool! She's turned down Hebe and Ariadne!'
'I've heard she had a lover once, Kallisto,
a clan child she would have died for.
They say, some traders stole the girl away.'
'No way? How come she never told us?'

'It's true. Artemis won her a place in the temple
through sheer cheek. But she was only there
a few turns of the moon, when she was tricked,
into leaving the *temenos*, forced aboard
a ship to marry some Mycenean lord.'

'I feel as cold as the snow on Ida...'
'How long ago was this?' 'Five years, I think.
The same time that her brother left –
they travelled with the same fleet
Poor Artemis was totally bereft.'

'Don't say she's never had a love since then?'
'I've heard she and Lady Dictynna are close.
Maybe they are lovers, who knows?'
'Don't think so. I reckon our hunting queen
is chaste as high Ida's untouched snows.'

'She's getting herself in a mess
over this trapping business though!
She'll never stop them, now they've learnt
to make these newfangled nets!
They catch more meat than any hunter gets.'

'It didn't used to be allowed –
trapping big animals was for cowards.
But since the people hunger now,
it's turning into a massive row.
Our Lady's defeat is on the cards.'

Rap attack

Chorus: modernisers

Art, you must appreciate
the people's hunger cannot wait
for land to naturally regenerate!
It will be too late.

We've got to innovate,
be creative, set the bait
in the trap, to get the food
to the plate. Simple.

How can you remonstrate?
You're the people's priestess,
so they say, well,
it wouldn't come amiss

if you used a bit of nouse.
If you don't like farming
and you don't like this,
just get real, sis!

You're gonna have a nerve
to tell folk they gotta starve
all on account of your principles!
Consider your priorities.

You think Potnia
wants hungry babies?
And get this too. This ain't
heresy and it ain't new.

It's straight from the Potnian
Old Testament: be divinely
different, make your eye be
innocent.

It's always been our credo.
No Potnian ever did
the same old
same old.

Sooo…we got to innovate,
be creative, set the bait
in the trap, to get the food
to the plate. Simple.

Taking a stand

Artemis

I won't live outside the sacred laws,
use our relations as convenience stores.

Our hunters take lives offered, as agreed
in trance, don't kill just from appetite and greed.

These traps are cowardly abominations
betraying a trust built for generations.

And I won't get drawn into 'them and us'
that attitude has resulted in this mess.

Charity will not help people rise above despair.
Handouts are no way of showing that we care.

What people need to live is opportunity –
recovery needs all our creativity!

While Knossos succumbs to foreign rule,
our treasures are exploited by mercenary fools.

Our 'Rulers' pile their platters with no regard
for hungry clans who live in their back yard

nor for the fact that they are harming
the balance of our land with all their farming.

Their herds destroy the medicine plants
that cleanse and heal and take us into trance.

One thing is obvious: everyone must eat
again more *horta*, much less meat.

Until such time, I'm taking leave of Knossos
to learn from kith and kin outside the *temenos*.

Beyond the Pale

Artemis

Actually, I'd needed an excuse to bugger off –
to get some space, sort my head out, as you might say,
go walkabout, get lost, to find myself again.
I'd lost Maya, and my brother, and worst of all
my soulmate and lover. Ignorant child that I was,
to think I could challenge the new disorder.
The temple is a ship without a mast: no one left
I can trust. But I had no plans to be an activist
or take that name they gave me: The People's Priestess.

Chorus 1

Crete's mountains would become her home:
destiny fulfilled, though goal unknown.

In forests and the untamed land
she'd find some true companions of her kind.

Girls wanting more challenges from life
than running a house as some man's wife,

girls who'd risked their lives to run away
discover strength by following a wilder way.

With Artemis they learnt the discipline to be free
a shaman's hard road to ecstasy –

healing through dance and journeying,
learning the rhythms of midwifery,

studying the subtleties of plant medicine,
the animals who'd be familiars for them.

Chorus 2

For nine long years they'd live to hunt and track –
till something in the stars called them back.

PART 3

The Return

Artemis

It was supposed to be Spring,
even allowing for continuing climate change.
But Winter wouldn't let go:

those glistening slopes that look
so ravishing from below
are full of lethal sinkholes under snow.

Even below the snow line, where
we'd plod over endless acres
of freezing scree,

we risked slithering into gorges,
dodging flash floods
and rockfalls from edges.

But the call to make this journey
couldn't have been clearer.
I'd fasted, dowsed, studied the stars.

I'd been guided in trance,
all the signs had agreed:
this change of destiny was ours.

It was the end of the great year
I'd spent away from Knossos. Now,
I'd been called back to the *temenos*.

So why was that Great Cow in the sky
pissing on us night and day,
lashing us with horizontal wind

that lifted the skirts of our tents
and soaked our goatskins so we had to
leave the stinking things to rot there?
And our footwear – well –

we tied them on with strips ripped
from whatever we could spare.

None of my girls complained
at the danger, aches and pains,
blisters and chilblains.

I'd told them life with me would be no picnic!
They gave their all and did me proud.
However, we were seriously exhausted.

Arrival

Artemis

Finally, Marti swore we were on course
to reach the place that evening.
We made a steep descent through clouds,
out onto sunlit slopes. Then it was
my poor girls went mad as hares –
anemones! Lilac, indigo, pink, cerise,
drifting as far as our eyes could see.

Soon after, through mountain pine
and budding chestnut trees,
a turquoise glimmer of the northern sea.
Spreading figs and stately planes
replaced holm oak, and massive
olive trunks threw purple lines
across the dappled tracks.

'Look at that mountain!' I whispered,
pointing at a profile chalked onto blue.
'Uncle Juktas! Asleep as usual
in the cobwebs of his breath.
They used to tell us it was the strong wine
brewed in his caves that made him sleepy.
But he always had half an eye open

for the children of Knossos. The temple
is right behind him, just out of sight.'
The wind had changed to a gentle westerly.
We found the simple sanctuary
as if we'd always known the way.
Only a crude *temenos* round a sacred tree:
fizzing with energy, but empty.

Not so much as a weedy child to meet us.
We waited, peered through the dusk,
fidgeted like calves at an empty trough,
and then...Holy Mother!...only

a High Priestess glided into sight,
like a full moon rising on a summer's night.
My girls near pissed themselves in shock an' awe:
they'd never seen a Priestess in full Power!

I'd always kept my light-body low key
since leaving Knossos, to save my energy.
Thought I'd done with glamour, but
heart now going like a goldsmith's hammer.
Cave black eyes I couldn't meet –
pulse racing to a crazy beat – who *is* she,
this Goddess towering over me?

When she draws her subtle body in,
she's still sensational in her skin:
taller than me with proud bare breasts
above snake-lacing on a cracking dress.
The warmth of her greeting verged on laughter:
I *must* have known a woman of such power.
I bow to hide my blushes, then have to rise –

the face before me blurrs, except the eyes
which twinkle like a little girl's: Kallisto!

She alone, Potnia be praised,
sees how completely I'm phased.
How this shape-shift had been wrought
I'd have to wait to learn, but thought,
only Knossos could have cooked
that raw child into this rare dish.
So, our roles have switched!

As in the spiral dance, we greet
each coming the other way:

I am all gristle now, she well-fed meat.
In my confusion, feel a great relief
as her next words seem to offer a reprieve:
inviting us to rest and recuperate
until the new moon rises tomorrow night.

I turn away to gather some composure
only to feel my wrist seized by Kallisto.

I follow like a child. Déjà vu.
Kids in the woods again, we two.

Meeting her match

Artemis

Kallisto! I soaked in the sweet, salt broth
of your body, and my own dried pods
swelled like ticks replete with blood.

I'd waited without knowing what I'd missed,
until I felt your arrows, unerring as my own,
your hunting muscles I would murder for.

'Come to my spring and bathe,'
you murmured, and we tumbled each other
on gravel in the icy night water.

'I've waited for you all my life,'
you hissed, tongue sending venomous
snakes to writhe in my molten belly.

Dawn had sucked the last light
from the embers of our fire,
before we succumbed to sleep.

We woke wrapped tight in your bearskin,
a high sun drawing steam from our bed.
Fused together, our limbs entwined

like ancient vines, inseparable.
A sense of being complete that I'd lost
at birth: Artemis not *parthenos*,

but part of a whole. Earth turning beneath,
heavens spinning above: I at the hub,
no longer at the edge, beyond the pale.

Taming the shrew

Kallisto

You've let yourself go, you know!

Girls

We've told her! She won't listen.

Kallisto

What do you look like? Daphne!
Come, we need you. Artemis, listen.

Daphne

Well, your hair's as dry as grass
for mattresses – try carob with hot beeswax,
with walnut to bring some colour back.
For your skin – ugh! Feel it! It's scaly!
Mix olive oil with avocado and a drop of iris:
apply warm at least twice daily.
Those nails – eat almonds for calcium.
And your heels – they have ravines in them!
Soak them in calendula tea, mixed
with some of your pee – still warm.
Then rub with ewe's butter every night.
And pick up some pumice – there's plenty,
it's free! As is my initial consultancy.

(Girls applause)

Kallisto

Maybe our guests would like a little pampering?
Why don't you take them to the spa, Daphne?
For a full treatment on me! Products included.
Tilissos has excellent new facilities: hot stones,
loofah scrubs, and the plunge pool is to die for.

The management's Athenian, but they're doing okay.
They learnt their massage from us, the traditional way.
Oils are top quality – well, as good as you get these days
– distilling techniques not what they used to be,
Too much demand, they cut corners.
I'd like to come with you: but I haven't the time.
Someone has to get this bratpack back on track!
C'mon girls, can't let the bow strings get slack!
I'll see you lot tonight, all shiny and bright. OK?'

Artemis

No, c'mon, honestly, it's not my thing...

Kallisto

It's quite compatible with rough and tumble,
my love! Just because I used to be a filthy brat,
doesn't mean that...

Girls

What does she mean, a filthy brat?

Artemis *(with relish)*

She had a mane of wiry hair, sort of dull charcoal,
so matted, mice could nest and breed in it.
It swept the ground, picking up sticks and leaves
as she crawled around on her hands and knees
like a monkey!

Girls

Not true! I don't believe it! Kallisto,
She's making it up, isn't she?

Kallisto

She's exaggerating, but it's kind of true.
We first made love covered in mud and blood
on the forest floor – and her from the temple too!
It was my adolescent rebellion:
I couldn't do real posh like her, so decided
to specialise in mucky, excel in rough.
Drove elders crazy with back-to-nature stuff.
Young Artemis, novice of Knossos,
tried to tame me, like everyone else.
Brought lotions and potions she and Old Maya
concocted. There was a rush on their health
and beauty products, but I held out for my place
at the temple, before I would touch the stuff!
Careful, Helena, your eyes are about to pop out!
And Io, take that grimace off your face!
Now off you ladies go to indulge yourselves,
these over-excited children need a race.

Chorus

So the lovers learnt to dance in time at last,
to teach and love and laugh in harmony.
And over time, they'd piece together the story,
of how the miracle had come to pass:
how a lost child had returned to glory,
overcome injury, self-loathing and despair,
all in the course of one Great Year.
But that's a tale for another time and place.
for times are changing fast at Knossos,
and our teachers must keep pace.

Catching up with the times

Kallisto

Artemis, this is our young priest Hyacinthos.
Tell her, flower, how Knossos has progressed
in the Great Year she's been absent –
see if she's impressed!

Hyacinthos

Well, Knossos is a happening place again.
All expats are graciously welcomed now,
no embarrassing questions asked
about background, education, spiritual persuasion:
all that counts is brass. That's pretty much official.
Helleno-sceptics are no longer mainstream.
The Potnian purists are seen as has-beens.
The real shamans, your sort, are underground.

Most nights, there's a gig in the bull court,
though bulls are now rarely seen.
The wine from our vineyards flows freely.
Myceneans, Athenians, even some Dorians,
all bring their chart-topping artists along
with their wheelers and dealers,
politicos, priests, and pretentious poets.

Musical tastes've changed too: lyras and lutes
are up there with our harpists and flutes.
In the harbour and city, street theatre:
wrestlers acrobats, jugglers, fire-walkers,
parades, all vying for space on the stage.
Ex-temple athletes and bull leapers join the fray:
their prowess proves quite lucrative.
Expat diners all agog, and able to pay.

Artemis

What are you doing fooling around at Knossos?
Why aren't the boys in the mountain retreats
doing kouretes training? Learning the ways
of your relations, following the spoors of the stag
and confounding the bulls. Dreaming with
plant medicines, drumming till you drop?

Hyacinthos

There have been...modifications,
madam, in the temple training programmes.
The kouretes' mountain exile has been
...well, rationalised, as they say.
There's an option on forestry skills.

We did have a weekend's drumming
at the Diktaeon cave. The bull masks
were dusted off, re-awakened, and we danced,
some of us even went into trance...then
the skies opened, lightening streaked
from peak to peak, some freaked out,
said Zeus was furious...so, bye bye
bull dancing.

A few try high mountain survival
to avoid the military route.
But marine battle strategy – compulsory.
Most opt for full military training
... incentives...and it's the in-thing to do.
Our boys pump up their muscles now with weights –
soft bellies and slim waists are out of date.
With foreign propaganda and peer pressure,
it's hard for guys – even girls I'd say –
to stay on Potnia's way. Few do.

Artemis

And you? Are you one of the few?

Hyacinthos

Yes, Lady. I've completed my training,
but most of my peers found it all too draining.
When my year group hit the hormones,
everyone's chasing tail, one kind or another.
It seems I'm considered pretty.
All my old playmates seemed to want
under my skirt. They wrote odes
to my ruddy lips and songs to my eyes.
I didn't want to give my prize
and managed to stay on course, until...
Well, first there was Hermes,
but of course that didn't last –
his tongue is as fleet as his feet,

he caught me and taught me
and was straightaway overseas.
He was born for the fast track – except
in the practise of pleasure!
I kept being drawn to Amnissos,
hoping he'd return with a fleet,
to sweep me off my feet again.
Even after I heard of his sojourn
on Cyprus, with a Priestess
by the name of Aphrodite...
I had no pride, but waited and watched,
pathetic as a dove whose mate
has been shot for the pot. Then...

Kallisto

It's alright flower, you can tell her.

Hyacinthos

I woke on the guesthouse roof one morning.
A brood of Athenian vessels sat fat on the water.
Crowds waiting excited like kids around honey.
Finally, in a posse of fawning sycophants,
not Hermes, but HE breezed up the ramps,
robed in white, his long hair catching the light
of the rising sun, like liquid gold rippling
its way to the mould. Their megastar.
His skin is flawless as snow on Mt Ida.
His smile dazzles: lit by its aura, you just melt
like the island of Dia when a rosy evening haze
is on her. Then when he plays on his lyra,
the notes take flight, carry you away
like a heavenly bird of prey. Oh Madam,
he preyed on us all! The novices were wet
for him alone. A troupe of our finest dancers
vied for his couch. A whole choir competed
to sing solo at his side. Knossos knelt
at his silk-slippered feet. No expense
was spared: parties were off the scale!
More meat was killed and fish was landed
than even the Solstice feasts commanded.

For he seems to have the light of Potnia in him.
He should have been Her consort, Her new Zan...
but some of his Hellenic hangers-on
boasted he was the darling of their Gods,
who'd claim him back, when he'd had enough of us.

Artemis

How could I not have guessed? Why not surprised?

Having it Made

Apollo

Call it karma, call it *moira*, call it fated.
I had to make my come-back sooner or later,
return to my roots and all that.
Wish I'd done it sooner, to be honest.
Knossos becoming quite the place
to show your face. Everyone
who's anyone is here, rubbing shoulders,
heads together, getting in on the action.
Reconstruction coming on apace.
Vultures, these merchant classes, though.
Sucking up to me, the royal scion.
But was fun to be welcomed home
as prodigal son. Especially now
those old-school rules have gone!

Beyond Narcissism

Artemis

So you fell for him too?

Hyacinthos

At first I just wanted to get away from it all, but I couldn't
spend every night with my ewes on the mountain.

My absence is noticed, my mothers fret, and Adrasteia
scowls ominously when we don't bat for our side.

So I show up to play, and one night as we're piping
a reel, I catch his gaze squarely on ME!

I blush, just manage to keep in the beat, but later
when I'm leaving, he only waylays me in a doorway,

complimenting my playing! Yeah, right, I think,
as he flashes his mile-wide smile and swaggers away.

But everything changed after that. Without even looking
I knew where he was in a room. I tried to avoid him,

of course: he was out of my realm, and worse,
a swerver, and a traitor. Why can't I fall for my sort?

A slim Keftian girl or boy? But, call me
a masochist, I was one of his bitches on heat.

Then one night under half a harvest moon
that hung in the summer sky like a broken plate,

he'd finished his set quite late, bowed and was gone.
I could stand it no longer and slipped from the throng

followed him out to the hot, perfumed night
and for his ears alone, I played my pipe.

The sounds of the night fell away. I knew he was near,
felt his breath on my neck, the world disappear...

We fled to my pastures and with the waxing moon.
For three days and nights our rhapsody grew.

I fed him on honey, milk warm from the ewes.
I washed him in dew. We played old tunes.

He was changed, my lady, I swear it's true,
he was...

Artemis

Keftian again? I believe you.
Soo...what happened to him? And you?
You look distraught, as if your spirit
had lost its thread, not been bedded by a god!

Hyacinthos

We lost each other, Ma'am.
We'd agreed to play together at the full moon rites.
For once, I looked forward to performing,
even the applause. I, too had changed,
eager to be seen with him, unashamed.
But Apollo went on ahead, while I followed
with some lambs for the full moon feast.
On the way, Greek guards accosted me:
big men, bearded, stinking of beer.
One held his massive hand against my cheek,
leering as a tradesman does at a vessel
he pretends to despise, to get it cheap.
I felt sick, as if I'd eaten the shaman's fungi.
A rough hand thrust under my tunic:
it wasn't a game. They meant me harm.
I had never liked wrestling, but now

my timing was immaculate. I twisted
like an eel and kicked backwards – hard
and accurate with my mountain clogs!
He howled and let go. I was off like an arrow.
They didn't try to follow. But when I got back
to Knossos, Apollo had left.

Artemis

So you got away? You were scarcely hurt?

Hyacinthus

But what had I done to be punished this way?
What is Potnia trying to say?
All we did was to honour Her…in sacred play…

Artemis

But you escaped, by Potnia's grace
with hardly a scratch on your beautiful butt!
Don't we give thanks when the scorpion
pricks but leaves no sting? Or when
a venomous snake hisses and does not strike?
Why are you not at Her altar, singing praises,
giving thanks for your life?
At least you had your hour of ecstasy!
Apollo has betrayed us all, especially me!

Hyacinthos *(sobs)*

Madam…

Artemis

Hyacinthos, you are a man now,
initiate and priest. What is your calling?

Hyacinthos

I am an exceptional musician, they say, Ma'am.

Artemis

And is that all they say? Don't you know
that a man must have more strings to his bow?
Potnia has nudged you, a little painfully.
You've had your wake-up call.
You told me they've cut back kouretes' training.
Yet you've just saved your skin by wrestling!
Children right now are slacking!
Missing lessons, skipping practise, am I right?
Get cracking! Tell your story! Take your authority!
Show them alternatives to the military.
Teach them how to face their fears,
and...know the beauty of their tears.

Hyacinthos

Yes Madam. Potnia be praised.

Family

Artemis

He dared to come back!
He was given a hero's welcome!

Kallisto

Hardly a hero, more like a Rock Star.
They just brought him back to taunt us,
wouldn't expect him to be led by the songlines
from stage to holy mountain, ignorant
of the power that still hums in our land.
Young Hyacinthus was part of Potnia's plan:
the love of a priestling, the winding way,
the moon. His armour was undone.
But he's their prize trophy:
their Cretan prodigy they've covered in glory.
They couldn't have him defect.

Artemis

He's a ship without a rudder,
belongs to the highest bidder.
Could never distinguish love from flattery.
Only I saw what was the matter with him!

Kallisto

Perhaps you overdid it, Timis!
you only talked about his weaknesses.
He needed your good opinion…

Artemis

Oh, c'mon! I mothered him from the beginning!

Kallisto

Exactly. You were his mother, sister and his brother too.
And you were more of a man than he was.
Because he couldn't run as fast or shoot as true
as you, you despised him. You think he didn't know that?

Artemis *(in tears)*

I loved him! He was the other half of myself!

Kallisto

The half you didn't want to own, that didn't measure up.

Artemis

I have to see him, Kal, before he leaves.
The harbour is but half a night from here.
The waning moon will light my way.

The last sibling spat

Apollo

Sister! To what do I owe the pleasure?

Artemis

How dare you try to run away again
when all the fates guided you back home?

Apollo

Listen, darling, they'll be calling me a God
long after your poor little brother
would only be a heap of crumbs
on the edge of an ossuary
if he stayed here in Crete.

Artemis

And deep in the minds of his people,
ready to be re-born when he was needed!

Apollo

Yes, well, I didn't get me such a great reception
the first time round, so I'd not place bets on the next.

Artemis

You were given more than your dues, Paian,
over and over. Then brought back, celebrated,
offered your rightful place, with a rare Keftian lover.
How could you stoop so low when you were raised so high?
In the holy embrace of Potnia's child – to betray that boy?

Apollo

If I'd stayed with that child one more night,
I'd have been lost forever on the mountain.
Lost in the night. Believe me, sister. Lost.

Artemis

Of course you'd have been lost!
That's the point. Don't you get it yet?
To be lost in love would have made you a man –
following the labyrinth's way, losing yourself to be found.
Everyone forgave you, even I would have forgiven you…

Apollo

Forgiven me for what, you uppity bitch?
What exactly was my original sin? Being a BOY?
Or going with those who recognised my worth?

Artemis

And flattered you! You became too vain
to make the surrenders required of a man!

Apollo

And WHO THE HELL ARE YOU TO TALK,
since you've so successfully avoided being a woman?

Artemis

I went through all the rites, Paian.
I avoided nothing.

Apollo

You never did! You skived off at the last post.
You dodged the *hieros gamos* and stayed a boy!

Artemis

That's a crazy thing to say!
It was you who disgraced yourself.
The son of great Leto refusing initiation!
You know that priesthood honours our autonomy
to follow our chosen paths – and sexuality!

Apollo

So how are the poor little bull calves
supposed to get their passports, if priestesses
are allowed to bunk off their initiations?
Bet it never happened in the good old days.
Anyway, I've heard on good authority
that the whole temple sorority
begged you to return to be the consort
of the king! Stability at Knossos guaranteed
by a marriage of interests, if you'd agreed...

Artemis

...to sleep with the enemy, you mean?

Apollo

If that's what you call being a Cretan Queen!

Artemis

The temple of Knossos knows neither
King or Queen – we have a High Priestess
with Zan, her man for a Great Year.

And that wasn't my *moira*.
I knew myself *parthenos* from being a girl.

Apollo

Well, beating a drum in the wilderness
wasn't my moira! Do me a favour –
it would have ruined my nails, dear.
A lutenist has to listen to his manicurist:
mine have to be long and smooth.
My hands are so sensitive!
How could I tear around in the forest,
making fire from sticks,
and clubbing boars to death?
It's disgusting. Can you really imagine me
living such a primitive life?

Artemis *(almost smiles)*

Put like that, no.
But must we always fight like this.

Apollo

If you keep constantly shrieking
at me like that harridan Adrasteia – yes!
I can't see how to avoid it!

Artemis

How dare you compare me to HER?

Apollo

Thought that would get a rise!
If the codpiece fits, wear it! Listen,
you know what it means, to be a God?
You take what you want. You and I, sis,

we're not as different as you think.
We both break the mould, go it alone.
We have our own way...why don't we...
just...have each other...what do you say?

Artemis

Oh, not that old song again!
You're my Goddamned twin brother!
Apollo

There's no law against it: it's happened before.
There's nothing to stop us having our...other lovers.
We should make an heir, of course – purely political.
Listen, the temple has lost the plot, you must see that.
Priestesses doped with opium, daft as bats, or escaped
from Knossos like you guys, rats from a sinking ship!

Artemis

You exaggerate!

Apollo

Greeks are all at one another's throats, arguing
like market traders about the price of land and labour,
barley, beans and oats – do me a favour!
Our precious perfumes are blended and degraded
Even our ancestors' graves are raided,
gold treasures melted down for coin.
Either the barbarians take over or we face them,
you and I, side by side on the throne of Knossos.
It's what we were born for, to reign together at this time:
create a Keftian-Olympian line.

Artemis

Don't make me laugh.

Apollo

You will be taken, you know, like it or not,
my little vixen. So you may as well
have me as a last ditch measure.
Or let the fool Minos take you as his whore.
Look what he's done to that stupid cow
Pasiphae: made her a laughing stock
throughout the world. You're next.
You're hunted, sister, not hunter now.
Your subversive teaching is a threat.
They'll track you down. And if you escape,
they'll go for your upstart tart.
Your little girls will be rounded up like rabbits,
cured of their strange notions and uncouth habits.
Your choices are running out – grab me while you can!
There's no place now for a woman without a man.

Artemis

Then I must be remembered as I am!
Go, move with the times if you must.
I'm going home to be with the one I trust.

Fate

Ship sounds, seafarers' voices.

The South Wind begins to blow! All aboard!
All aboard! Hoist sails and man the oars!

Artemis *(breathless)*

Wait! I'm coming with you!

Apollo

What? Back already? You'd leave Crete?
Where's your girlfriend?
                         (Laughs gleefully)

Artemis

Kallisto died by her own hand to escape rape
by the men you sent to take revenge on me.
Now nothing can ever touch her constancy:
she shines as Arcturus among the stars.

    (The rumble of an earthquake and then a hiss of flames rising from Knossos.)

Apollo

What's that?

Artemis

Knossos burning. Look how the flames are fanned
by the same south wind that fills our sails

Apollo

You knew? My Gods, you knew!

Artemis

The work of prophecy never left the temple,
just descended to the dark.
Knossos will never rise again:
but a labyrinth will always leave
its ghostly pathway for those
who know to walk between the worlds.

Chorus

Men thought they could marry Potnia to their powers,
raise her up to sit among their Gods.
But Potnia is the drawing down of power:
we were her feet, her hands, her songs of praise,
we were the living mirror of her face.

Postlude

Artemis

I next showed up in Sparta,
a Goddess famous for my bloody altars.
Men would live in fear of being flayed
if harsh but just laws were disobeyed.

Young girls were my companions:
mountainsides their schools,
bearskins their uniforms,
natural laws their rules.

Apollo

Sis is insufferable,
still causing trouble,
but somewhere along the line
things got in a bit of a muddle.

All that proportion and harmony,
bright lights and glory,
as time went by, did seem
to tell a different story.

What's shiny outside can be vile inside.
I know it's been said before,
but it's got really hard to tell
what's civilised any more.

Explanatory notes on names and places
(in order of first mention)

Knossos: The temple/palace at the centre of the Minoan civilisation in ancient Crete and going back to Neolithic times. Surviving and being rebuilt after many earthquakes, it was finally destroyed some time later than the Theran volcanic eruption (c1450) that destroyed many of the Minoan temples. One theory is that the island of Dia, which lies offshore to the north of Knossos and present day Heraklion, protected the area from the worst impact of tsunami.

Thera: Island now known as Santorini blown apart by the volcano that destroyed much of Crete, and caused widespread climate change, around 1450 BC.

Keftiou/Keftian: Older name for Crete/Cretan.

Eileuthia: Ancient Goddess of childbirth, whose sacred cave is near the harbour of Knossos (and Heraklion airport!). She was said to have enrolled the help of newborn Artemis in the delivery of her brother, leading to Artemis being known as the Goddess of midwives.

Leto: Mother of the twins, Artemis and Apollo, who disappeared after carrying them to Knossos from the sacred cave of Eileuthia on the night of the volcano.
Leto in myth: *Was originally a daughter begot on a moon Goddess by Intelligence. When Zeus tricked her into coupling, she was pursued by his wife Hera until she gave birth in a place where the sun never shone, the exact location of which was long disputed. I have continued the tradition of disagreement by putting their birthplace in a Cretan cave. Some years after this decision, two statuettes of Artemis and Apollo were found at Aptera, a site near a famous cave of Artemis in NW Crete, showing that there had been a 'cult' to the pair there well into the Greek era.*

kouretes: Young male initiates at Knossos, dancers and drummers.
kouretes in myth*: They protected the young Zeus from being murdered by his father Kronos by drumming to drown out the baby's crying in the*

cave where he was hiding. They are pictured in dancing rituals wearing bulls' masks, and were probably also the bull-leapers. Their name means devotees of the triple Goddess.

Mycenean: Greeks from Mycenae, who, though militaristic, adopted much cultural refinement from Minoans, with whom they had close trading links. They later colonised the devastated island, transforming the society and leading the way for more warlike Greek invaders, such as Dorians.

Potnia: The name of the Goddess inscribed on tablets in Knossos as a divinity to whom offerings were made. It means Powerful or Potent Lady. What we call the Minoan culture could more accurately be described as the Potnian culture.

Zan: Father of Artemis and Apollo, but known as Uncle Zan to them as fatherhood was not recognised. A great hunter, who stayed in a position of authority for a Great Year (9 years) after Leto's disappearance.
Zan in myth: *Male consort of the High Priestess in Crete, probably for a Great Year (9 years), sometimes see as a fertility God. Believed to be the precursor of Zeus.*

Diktynna: Pre-Greek name for the Goddess in Crete, still worshipped into historic times, meaning She of the nets (or networker!).

Pasiphae: Ancient Goddess of Crete, associated with the great cow, whose consort was the sacred bull, and whose udders gave us the milky way. The Greeks made her the errant wife of Minos, who lusted after a bull and birthed a monster.

Minos: King of Crete in Homer and Greek mythology, but if he existed it was after what is now called the Minoan era.

Zeus: Later Greek deification of Zan.
Zeus in myth: *Head of the Olympians, whose pursuits and rapes of more ancient Goddesses produced many of the other Greek deities, including Artemis and Apollo.*

Glossary

Krassi: Cretan wine.
horta: wild greens still eaten in Crete today.
temenos: the sacred area surrounding the temple. The region of modern Heraklion which includes Knossos is still called Temenos today.
hieros gamos: sacred marriage of Goddess (or Priestess) and consort in ancient world.
moira: personal fate or path.
parthenos: word usually translated as virgin, but meaning apart, or one-unto-herself, or even unmarried.
Arcturoi: girls who served Artemis dressed in bearskins in later Greek mythology.

Thanks to

Many people who have helped inspire and support this book. Bernadine Evaristo whose verse novels excited me into turning my then novel into verse, and who also applauded my early efforts. Jay Griffiths, whose courage and inspiring books in defence of the wild epitomise for me the Artemis archetype in the world today; and whose encouragement has helped me finish. The authors of all the many books I've read about the ancient Goddesses and pre-patriarchal societies, in particular Ann Baring and Jules Cashford for *The Myth of the Goddess*, and Susan Evasdaughter whose early pamphlets first led me to the sacred sites of Crete all those years ago. And to all the women who have made pilgrimages in Crete with me since. And to those who have read versions of the text aloud to bring it alive and thus helped it survive. To my husband for bearing with me, and keeping faith as the writing morphed over the years. And last but very importantly, the amazing Kate Garrett for loving it enough to publish it. Thank you.

About the Author

Cora Greenhill has been making pilgrimages to Crete since 1984, when she started her exploration of the pre-patriarchal 'Minoan' world. She found this gave her feminism an embodied depth that she expressed through dance and poetry. She has since taken many dance groups to creatively respond to the power of the Cretan caves and ancient sites where 'the veil between the worlds is thin'.
She taught Gabrielle Roth's 5 Rhythm dancework for over 20 years, after a career teaching literature and counselling.
She and her husband now have a home in Crete. In England they have lived in The Peak District near Sheffield for 30 years. She teaches poetry and writing and hosts Writers in The Bath in Sheffield. She wants a gap year travelling to World Music Festivals.

Also by Cora Greenhill

Dreadful Work (1989)
Deep in Time (1999)
The Point of Waking (Oversteps Books, 2013)
Far from Kind (Pindrop Press, 2016)